Anti-Inflammatory Drinks

Heal Your Immune System and Fight Inflammation with These 75 Smoothies, Teas, Juices, and Much More!

Stephanie Bennett

TABLE OF CONTENTS

INTRODUCTION

Inflammation is your immune system's response to injury or unwanted microbes in your body. It is a natural process and vital part of your body's healing process. When inflammation becomes systemic and chronic, however, it becomes a problem, and measures need to be taken. This type of inflammation serves no purpose, and can cause a lot of harm to the body.

As a nutritionist, I have clients suffering from a wide spectrum of health issues, and inflammation is easily one of the most common issues. Some of these clients are in constant pain, often excruciating. Migraines are a regular occurrence, and they don't sleep too well either. Their energy reserves always seem depleted and even sleep doesn't help, even if they manage to get a few good hours in.

I always suggest these clients to get a blood test for C-reactive protein if they haven't got one already, and if you feel you suffer from any symptoms of inflammation, I suggest you go to a nearby lab and get this blood test done right away. Chances are that your C-reactive protein levels are higher than normal, and the best way to manage this is diet. Shouldn't be hard though, considering how delicious anti-inflammatory foods are! Even if you do not suffer from chronic and systemic inflammation, incorporating anti-inflammatory foods in your diet will be one of the best decisions you will make in your life. You will notice the difference when you start. Your energy levels will be much higher, your mood will be uplifted, and you will feel more alive, in general.

This book has a LOT of recipes, and not every recipe might work for you. For example, if you're allergic to dairy or gluten, the recipes containing those ingredients will cause more harm than good. However, substitutions are possible for all of these, so you will be fine following this book as long as you keep an eye on the ingredients and use a bit of creativity where you have to! Once you understand the fundamentals of the diet, you will be fully equipped to create your own recipes from scratch!

In this book, you will learn all about the ingredients that are alleviate inflammation, and those that aggravate it, so you can make an educated guess for what's the best recipe for you, and what's the worst, even if you're out eating at a restaurant.

CAUSES OF CHRONIC INFLAMMATION

Medical science is striving to pinpoint the causes of chronic inflammation, and according to the Autoimmunity Research Foundation, numerous possible causes have been identified. This knowledge has mainly been derived from observational studies in which researchers can find correlation, though correlation does not equate to causation. Which is to say that while causes are identified by the studies, there is no scientifically proven concrete link between causes and outcomes. This uncertainty is an integral part of epidemiological studies, but they can still provide some very useful information.

Suggested causes for widespread chronic inflammation include:

- Antibiotic overuse and misuse (including in the food supply and through prescribed medications)
- Dietary factors (processed foods, unbalanced essential fatty acids, and chemical additives, among others)
- Environmental factors (endocrine disrupters and pesticides, among others)
- Use of substances (medications) that suppress immune responses, such as anti-inflammatories, antibacterial agents, and corticosteroids

In addition,* Medical News Today *(MNT) notes other factors that may play a role in chronic inflammation, including:

- Autoimmune diseases
- Obesity
- Poor sleep quality and sleep deprivation

CHRONIC INFLAMMATORY DISEASES

The research goes on but quite a few diseases have been linked to chronic inflammation. In this section, we will take a look at some of these.

AUTOINFLAMMATORY DISEASE

According to the National Institutes of Health's (NIH) National Institute of Arthritis and Musculoskeletal and Skin Diseases (NIAMS), autoinflammatory disease is a rather new class that is quite unlike autoimmune disease, although the names are rather similar and they share some features. Autoimmune diseases are caused by the immune system attacking healthy tissue, leading to chronic inflammation. The reason for this is not fully understood by science just yet.

Autoinflammatory diseases can cause intense, chronic inflammation that can lead to symptoms such as fever and joint swelling. A few common diseases in this category are:

- Behçet's disease
- Chronic Atypical Neutrophilic Dermatosis with Lipodystrophy and Elevated Temperature (CANDLE)
- Deficiency of the Interleuken-1 Receptor Agonist (DIRA)
- Familial Mediterranean Fever (FMF)
- Neonatal Onset Multisystem Inflammatory Disease (NOMID)
- Tumor Necrosis Factor Receptor-Associated Periodic Syndrome (TRAP)

AUTOIMMUNE DISEASE

NIAMS says that autoimmune diseases also have a chronic inflammatory component to them. When your body sees its own healthy tissue as an intruder, it attacks it. Inflammation is one of the key signs of autoimmune disease, although, depending on the disease, other symptoms might be exhibited too.

More than 80 autoimmune diseases have been identified at the time of writing this book, and some of the most common ones are listed below:

- Addison's disease
- Ankylosing spondylitis
- Celiac disease
- Crohn's disease
- Endometriosis
- Fibromyalgia
- Grave's disease
- Hashimoto's disease
- Interstitial cystitis
- Juvenile (type 1) diabetes
- Juvenile arthritis
- Lupus
- Lyme disease (chronic)
- Multiple sclerosis
- Psoriasis

- Rheumatoid arthritis
- Scleroderma
- Ulcerative colitis
- Vitiligo

CARDIOVASCULAR DISEASE

The American Heart Association notes that while it isn't currently established that inflammation causes cardiovascular disease (diseases of the heart and blood vessels), it is usually present, particularly in arteries of people suffering from this kind of a disease. Multiple factors are associated with heart disease, such as tobacco use, high blood pressure, and high levels of "bad" cholesterol called low-density lipoprotein (LDL), etc., so managing these is key to preventing and managing cardiovascular diseases.

TYPE 2 DIABETES AND OBESITY

An article in the May 2, 2005 issue of the Journal of Clinical Investigation studied the link between type 2 (adult onset) diabetes, inflammation, and stress, and found a close correlation between inflammation and type 2 diabetes, mostly triggered by obesity. This research suggests that obesity activates multiple chemical responses in the body that result in extensive inflammation, and this inflammation further causes metabolic disorders like type 2 diabetes.

MANAGING CHRONIC INFLAMMATION

With advances in medical science, we have quite a few options for managing chronic inflammation. Some of the most popular options today are as follows.

NSAIDS

Nonsteroidal anti-inflammatory drugs (NSAIDs) such as ibuprofen or naproxen sodium (Aleve) are often recommended by health experts for managing and treating inflammation. However, these can potentially cause side effects, especially when used in the long term.

CORTICOSTEROIDS

These synthetic steroids are administered both orally and externally, and are great at suppressing the body's immune response. However, these too can cause side effects in the long run.

HERBAL REMEDIES

Minor inflammation can be managed by simple herbal remedies containing anti-inflammatory ingredients like turmeric and ginger. Combining turmeric with black pepper, coconut oil, or quercetin increases its bioavailability, thus making it easier for the body to absorb it.

LIFESTYLE CHANGES

Simple lifestyle changes such as exercise, yoga, meditation, better sleep, losing weight, stress reduction techniques, etc. can go a long way in managing inflammation.

ANTI-INFLAMMATORY DIET

The anti-inflammatory diet is a fairly new concept, and research is still going on. However, a review in the December 2010 issue of **Nutrition in Clinical Practice** notes an anti-inflammatory eating pattern which balances the ratio of essential fatty acids (omega-3 to omega-6 fatty acids) and consists mainly of fresh fruits, vegetables, legumes, and whole grains while reducing saturated fats (such as fats from meat) and maximizing monounsaturated fats (such as olive oil), is much better at managing inflammation than a typical western diet.

ANTI-INFLAMMATORY EATING HABITS

You are what you eat. Eat good, look good, feel good. Eat trash, look like trash, feel like trash.

FIGHTING INFLAMMATION THROUGH DIET

The anti-inflammatory diet has a very simple concept. When you plan your meals, you maximize the ingredients that reduce inflammation, and minimize/eliminate the ingredients that aggravate inflammation. Though, this is easier said than done.

We live in a world where everything, even food, is available at the flick of your finger. We are surrounded by delicious processed food with chemical additives, preservatives, and unhealthy fats. When such good taste comes with such high convenience, it is easy to give in.

However, if you do manage to overcome your urges, and decide to eat healthy, I'll tell you what you need to look for. Head to a nearby farmers' market and pick out fresh anti-inflammatory ingredients. Some of the most potent anti-inflammatory ingredients are listed under the next heading.

ANTI-INFLAMMATORY INGREDIENTS

Not all ingredients are created equal when it comes to the anti-inflammatory diet. Some are simply better and more potent than the others. I am a woman of science, and medical research has revealed some of the best ingredients for managing inflammation. If you're serious about this diet, you will do well to have all these ingredients on hand at all times.

BELL PEPPERS

Bell peppers—particularly red bell peppers—are a great source of antioxidants and capsaicin, both of which are exceptional at fighting inflammation. Add them to recipes containing turmeric for an anti-inflammatory bomb. They also contain quercetin, which enhances your body's absorption of anti-inflammatory curcumin. Be careful using these if you're sensitive to nightshades though.

BROCCOLI

High in fiber and immunity-boosting antioxidants like vitamin C, broccoli is a potent inti-inflammatory ingredient.

KALE

This vegetable is loaded with fiber and antioxidants.

SPINACH

Loaded with antioxidants like vitamin C and K, spinach is great at fighting inflammation.

TOMATOES

As long as you're not sensitive to nightshades, tomato is amazing at fighting inflammation, thanks to the lycopene contained within.

BLUEBERRIES

Blueberries are rich in antioxidants, and augment your immune system while fighting inflammation. Oh, and they taste absolutely amazing!

SALMON AND OTHER FATTY FISH

A good balance of essential fatty acids (omega-3 and omega-6 fatty acids) is absolutely vital to combat inflammation. Omega-3 fatty acids are anti-inflammatory, while omega-6 fatty acids are pro-inflammatory. Functional medicine specialist Chris Kresser notes that the perfect ratio of omega-6 fatty acids to omega-3 fatty acids is 1:1 or 2:1. The problem with the typical western diet is that this ratio is really unbalanced. The omega-6 fatty acid is so high in the western diet that the ratio can be as bad as 25:1! To counter this, supplemental fish oil rich in omega-3 fatty acids can be taken, or better yet, a diet rich in salmon and other fatty fish can be taken. These fish taste absolutely amazing, and are great anti-inflammatory ingredients!

NUTS

Nuts rich in omega-3 fatty acids are best. Some of these are: walnuts, cashews, almonds, pecans, etc. These have a high calorie density, so eat in moderation if you're looking to lose weight.

CINNAMON

Cinnamon contains cinnamaldehyde, which, according to an article in the January 2008 issue of **Food and Chemical Toxicology**, is a great at fighting inflammation.

GARLIC

One of the most potent anti-inflammatory ingredients, garlic has been used in home remedies since ancient times. Modern science too has now confirmed that garlic enhances the immune system, and is one of the best anti-inflammatory ingredients out there.

GINGER

Ginger adds an amazing flavor to whichever dish it is added, and boasts potent anti-inflammatory properties to boot!

ROSEMARY

This fragrant and flavorful herb is a potent anti-inflammatory ingredient. It goes especially well in a non-vegetarian dish.

TURMERIC

Turmeric contains curcumin, which many studies have concluded is great at fighting inflammation.

EXTRA-VIRGIN OLIVE OIL

EVOO is loaded with healthy fats, and contains oleocanthal, which is a potent anti-inflammatory compound.

GREEN TEA

Green tea is loaded with antioxidants, enhances the immune system, and has anti-inflammatory properties.

INGREDIENTS TO WATCH OUT FOR

While a certain ingredient might reduce inflammation in one person, it might do the exact opposite for another. Below is the list of a few ingredients that are common allergens, and if a certain recipe in this book doesn't help with inflammation, try eliminating these ingredients first.

The anti-inflammatory diet for every person will be a little different, and you are the only person who can find what ingredients suit you best. Below is the list of ingredients to watch out for:

- Dairy Products: A lot of people are allergic to casein, whey, and lactose. All three are contained in milk, and if you're allergic to even one of these, substitute dairy for nondairy alternatives such as almond milk or hemp milk.
- Eggs: This is an allergen that is hard to substitute in most cases. If you're baking, eggs can be replaced by flax eggs. Flax eggs can be made by mixing 1 tbsp ground flaxseed with 2½ tablespoons water and allowing to rest for 5 minutes until thick. This substitutes one egg in baking recipes.
- Fish: If you're allergic to fish, try shellfish instead. If you're allergic to that too, try chicken instead. Try tofu in fish recipes for a vegan dish. Soy sauce is a great alternative to fish sauce.
- Gluten: Gluten is one of the most common allergens out there. This protein is found in wheat, barley, etc. Two of my favorite gluten free grains are millet and quinoa.

- Nightshades: If you're sensitive to these, you should avoid eating tomatoes, tomatillos, goji berries, eggplant, bell peppers, chile peppers, and potatoes. Two alternatives are onions are garlic, but nightshades can never truly be substituted.
- Peanuts: Peanut allergy is quite common. It is a legume so substitute it with a nut you like and are not allergic to.
- Soy: If you're allergic to soy, you will need to read labels of all food items you buy. Tofu can be substituted by chicken, while soy sauce can be replaced by a spice blend of your choice.
- Tree Nuts: Tree such as almonds, walnuts, pecans, cashews, Brazil nuts, macadamia nuts, etc. are allergens to some. Try peanuts or a different nut you're not allergic to instead.
- Wheat: Another common allergen, wheat is easily replaced by buckwheat or rice flour.

THE COMPLETE ANTI-INFLAMMATORY FOOD LIST

BEVERAGES

POTENTIAL PRO-INFLAMMATORY INGREDIENTS (AVOID/MINIMIZE)

Soft drinks, sweetened (with sugar or artificial sweetener) || Soda, regular || Soda, diet || Milk, dairy || Liquor, hard || Liqueurs || Juice, sweetened || Energy drinks || Beer || Artificially or sugar sweetened drinks

INGREDIENTS THAT REDUCE INFLAMMATION (EAT THESE)

Wine (limit 4 oz.) || Kombucha || Coffee || Chai (with nondairy milk and no sugar)

POTENT ANTI-INFLAMMATORY FOODS (EAT A LOT)

Water || Tea (Particularly Green Tea)

CONDIMENTS

POTENTIAL PRO-INFLAMMATORY INGREDIENTS (AVOID/MINIMIZE)

Vinaigrette (store-bought) || Teriyaki sauce (store-bought) || Salsa, with sugar || Salad dressing || Mayonnaise (store-bought) || Ketchup || Cocktail sauce || Barbecue sauce

INGREDIENTS THAT REDUCE INFLAMMATION (EAT THESE)

Worcestershire sauce || Wasabi || Vinegar, all kinds || Vinaigrette (homemade) || Tomato paste || Teriyaki sauce, sugar-free (homemade) || Tamari || Tahini || Soy sauce || Salsa, sugar-free || Mustard, ground || Mustard, Dijon || Miso || Mayonnaise (homemade) || Hot sauce, sugar-free || Horseradish, prepared, sugar-free || Fish sauce, sugar-free || Anchovy paste

DAIRY AND DAIRY ALTERNATIVES

POTENTIAL PRO-INFLAMMATORY INGREDIENTS (AVOID/MINIMIZE)

Whipped cream || Sour cream || Nondairy creamer || Kefir, cow's milk || Ice cream || Heavy (whipping) cream || Half-and-half || Goat's milk || Cow's milk (all types) || Cheese, dairy (all types)

INGREDIENTS THAT REDUCE INFLAMMATION (EAT THESE)

Yogurt, Greek || Yogurt, dairy || Yogurt, coconut, plain, unsweetened || Yogurt, almond, plain, unsweetened || Soymilk, unsweetened || Kefir, water || Hemp milk, unsweetened || Coconut milk, lite, unsweetened || Coconut milk, full-fat, unsweetened || Almond milk, unsweetened

FATS AND OILS

POTENTIAL PRO-INFLAMMATORY INGREDIENTS (AVOID/MINIMIZE)

Vegetable oil || Sunflower oil || Soybean oil || Shortening || Sesame oil || Safflower oil || Peanut oil || Palm oil || Margarine || Lite olive oil || Hydrogenated oils || Corn oil || Canola oil || Butter

INGREDIENTS THAT REDUCE INFLAMMATION (EAT THESE)

Macadamia oil || Coconut oil || Avocado oil

POTENT ANTI-INFLAMMATORY FOODS (EAT A LOT)

Extra-Virgin Olive Oil

FRUITS

POTENTIAL PRO-INFLAMMATORY INGREDIENTS (AVOID/MINIMIZE)

Processed juices with added sugar || Canned fruit in syrup

INGREDIENTS THAT REDUCE INFLAMMATION (EAT THESE)

Yuzu || Watermelon || Ugli fruit || Tayberry || Tangerine || Tamarind || Strawberry || Star fruit || Satsuma || Santa Claus melon || Salmonberry || Red currant || Raspberry || Raisin || Quince || Prunes || Prickly pear || Pomelo || Pomegranate || Pluot || Plum || Plantain || Pineapple || Persimmon || Persian melon || Pear || Peach || Passionfruit || Papaya || Orange || Olives || Nectarine || Mulberry || Marionberry || Mangosteen || Mango || Mandarin || Lychee || Lime ||

Lemon || Kumquat || Kiwi || Jackfruit || Huckleberry || Horned melon || Honeydew || Guava || Grapefruit || Grape || Gooseberry || Goji berry || Galia (melon) || Fig || Elderberry || Durian || Dragon fruit || Date || Currant || Cranberry || Coconut || Clementine || Chokecherry || Cherry || Charentais (melon) || Casaba melon || Cantaloupe || Canary melon || Breadfruit || Boysenberry || Blood orange || Blackcurrant || Blackberry || Banana || Avocado || Asian pear || Apricot || Apple || Acai

POTENT ANTI-INFLAMMATORY FOODS (EAT A LOT)

Blueberries

GRAINS AND STARCHES

*INGREDIENTS THAT MAY
TRIGGER INFLAMMATION (AVOID/MINIMIZE)*

Wheat, refined || Rice, white || Potato starch || Pasta || Oatmeal, instant, with sugar || Flour, white || Cereal || Bread, white || Baked goods (bread, cookies, donuts, pies, etc.)

INGREDIENTS THAT REDUCE INFLAMMATION (EAT THESE)

Wild rice || Wheat, whole || Wheat, cracked || Teff || Rye || Rice, brown || Quinoa || Oats, rolled || Millet || Kamut || Farro || Cornstarch || Corn || Bulgur || Buckwheat || Barley || Arrowroot || Amaranth

MEATS, POULTRY, FISH, AND PROTEINS

POTENTIAL PRO-INFLAMMATORY INGREDIENTS (AVOID/MINIMIZE)

Whey protein || Trout, fried || Shrimp, fried || Scallops, fried || Sausage || Salami || Pork, ground || Liver (all types) || Lamb, rib chops || Lamb, rack || Kidney (all types) || Hot dogs || Heart (all types) || Ham || Gizzards || Foie gras || Fish, fried || Farmed seafood || Deli meats || Cured meats || Chicken, fried || Catfish, fried || Brains (all types) || Bologna || Beef, rib eye || Beef, prime rib || Beef, New York strip || Beef, feedlot || Bacon

INGREDIENTS THAT REDUCE INFLAMMATION (EAT THESE)

Venison || Turkey, free-range, skinless || Tilapia, wild-caught || Sturgeon, wild-caught || Snapper || Skate || Shrimp || Scallops || Razor clams || Pork, top loin roast || Pork, tenderloin (preferably pastured) || Pork, sirloin roast || Pork, rib chop || Pork, center loin chop || Pork, boneless top loin chop || Orange roughy || Mussels || Lamb, very lean cuts || Halibut || Elk || Eggs || Duck, free-range, skinless || Cod || Clams || Chicken, free-range, skinless || Catfish, wild-caught || Bison, lean || Beef, lean or very lean || Bass, wild-caught || Anchovy

POTENT ANTI-INFLAMMATORY FOODS (EAT A LOT)

Salmon (and other fatty fish including tuna, mackerel, sardines, and trout)

NUTS, SEEDS, AND LEGUMES

INGREDIENTS THAT REDUCE INFLAMMATION (EAT THESE)

Walnuts, raw || Sunflower seeds || Soybeans || Sesame seeds || Poppy seeds || Pistachios, raw || Pinto beans || Pine nuts || Pecans, raw || Peas, sugar snap || Peas, split || Peas, snow || Peas, green || Peas, black-eyed || Peanuts, raw || Peanut butter || Macadamia nuts, raw || Lima beans || Lentils || Kidney beans || Hazelnuts, raw || Flaxseed || Fava beans || Cocoa beans (dark chocolate, cocoa powder) || Chickpeas (garbanzo beans) || Chia seeds || Cashews, raw || Brazil nuts, raw || Black beans || Almonds, raw || Almond butter || Adzuki beans

POTENT ANTI-INFLAMMATORY FOODS (EAT A LOT)

NUTS

SWEETENERS

POTENTIAL PRO-INFLAMMATORY INGREDIENTS (AVOID/MINIMIZE)

Xylitol || Syrup, brown rice, corn, high fructose corn, maple (artificial), simple || Sugar, brown and powdered || Sugar alcohols || Sucralose (Splenda) || Sorbitol || Saccharine || Molasses, refined || Mannitol || Erythritol || Aspartame (NutraSweet) || Agave nectar || Acesulfame-K (Acesulfame potassium)

INGREDIENTS THAT REDUCE INFLAMMATION (EAT THESE)

Stevia || Maple syrup, pure || Honey

VEGETABLES

POTENTIAL PRO-INFLAMMATORY INGREDIENTS (AVOID/MINIMIZE)

Zucchini || Yam || Watercress || Water chestnut || Wakame || Turnip greens || Turnip || Tomatoes, canned (sugar-free) || Tomato sauce (sugar-free) || Tomatillo || Swiss chard || Sweet potato || Sunchoke || Sprouts || Spinach || Spaghetti squash || Shallots || Scallions || Rutabaga || Rapini || Purslane || Pumpkin || Potatoes || Pea pods || Pattypan squash || Parsnip || Onions || Okra || Nori || Nopales || Mustard greens || Mushrooms || Lettuce (all types) || Kohlrabi Leeks || Jicama

INGREDIENTS THAT REDUCE INFLAMMATION (EAT THESE)

Hearts of palm || Grape leaves || Frisée || Fennel || Endive || Eggplant || Edamame || Dulse || Cucumber || Corn || Collard greens || Chayote || Celery || Celeriac (celery root) || Cauliflower || Carrots || Cabbage || Butternut squash || Brussels sprouts || Broccolini || Broccoli rabe || Bok choy || Beets || Beet greens || Beans, green || Asparagus || Arugula || Artichoke || Acorn squash

POTENT ANTI-INFLAMMATORY FOODS (EAT A LOT)

Tomatoes || spinach || kale || broccoli || bell peppers

HERBS, AND SPICES

POTENTIAL PRO-INFLAMMATORY INGREDIENTS (AVOID/MINIMIZE)

Table salt || Spice blends with sugar || Seasoning salt || Garlic salt

INGREDIENTS THAT REDUCE INFLAMMATION (EAT THESE)

Vanilla bean || Thyme || Tarragon || Sumac || Spearmint || Salt, Himalayan pink and sea || Sage || Saffron || Rhubarb || Red pepper flakes || Radish || Radicchio || Pepper (black) || Parsley || Paprika || Oregano || Orange zest || Onion powder || Nutmeg || Mustard seed || Mustard powder || Mint || Marjoram || Mace || Lime zest || Lemongrass || Lemon zest || Lemon pepper || Lavender || Juniper berry || Horseradish || Herbes de Provence || Garam masala || Galangal || Fenugreek || Fennel seed || Dill || Curry powder || Cumin || Coriander || Cilantro || Chives || Chipotle || Chinese five-spice powder || Chile peppers || Chamomile || Celery salt || Cayenne || Cassia || Caraway || Bay leaves || Basil || Asafoetida || Anise, star || Anise || Allspice

POTENT ANTI-INFLAMMATORY FOODS (EAT A LOT)

TURMERIC || ROSEMARY || GINGER || GARLIC || CINNAMON

PANTRY ESSENTIALS

If you're serious about the anti-inflammatory diet, you will do well to make the following ingredients a staple in your pantry:

CANNED ITEMS

- Tomatoes, crushed
- Tomatoes, chopped
- Red bell peppers, roasted, in oil
- Coconut milk, lite
- Broth, vegetable, no salt added
- Broth, chicken, no salt added

HERBS AND SPICES

- Turmeric, ground
- Thyme, dried
- Salt, Himalayan pink or sea
- Rosemary, dried
- Red pepper flakes
- Peppercorns
- Oregano, dried
- Onion powder
- Nutmeg, ground
- Ginger, ground
- Garlic powder
- Curry powder
- Cinnamon, ground
- Chili powder

NUTS, SEEDS, LEGUMES, AND GRAINS

- Sunflower seeds
- Sesame seeds, toasted
- Rice, brown, cooked
- Quinoa
- Peanut butter
- Lentils, canned

- Chickpeas, canned
- Beans, kidney, canned
- Beans, black, canned
- Almond butter

OILS, VINEGARS, AND CONDIMENTS

- Vinegar, apple cider
- Soy sauce, low-sodium (or gluten-free or tamari)
- Olive oil, extra-virgin
- Mustard, Dijon

SUGAR, BAKING INGREDIENTS, AND FLOURS

- Vanilla extract
- Sugar, brown
- Stevia
- Milk, almond, hemp, or rice, unsweetened
- Maple syrup, pure
- Honey
- Green tea
- Cocoa powder, unsweetened
- Arrowroot powder (or cornstarch)

TIPS AND TRICKS

Here are a few suggestions I give to my clients to make it easier for them to cook the food, and stick to the diet:

- Weekly Diet Plans Work. If you think too much ahead, things will be hard. Plan for a week, or even less. Make a meal plan using the recipes in this book, and make a shopping list. Shopping only for the ingredients you'll be using in the following week will ensure that they stay fresh, and your brain stays relatively stress-free.
- Cook in Large Batches. If you're lazy like me and wouldn't like to cook three times every day, try cooking a LOT. This only works for dishes that store well in the fridge. Take a serving size out of the fridge, heat using a microwave, eat, repeat.
- Have Fun With Leftovers. Leftovers are a great opportunity to let your imagination run wild and invent a new recipe tailored to your personal taste!

- Veggies are Love. Buy lots of fresh vegetables when you're at a grocery store. Better yet, take a stroll through a farmers' market near you.
- Try Different Cooking Methods. Depending on how much time you have, and when you want to eat, a different cooking method might make the work easier. Slow cooking, for example, is great for someone who has a day job and would like to come back home to a home cooked meal, without another home cook.
- Prepare and Shop on Weekends and Holidays. If you have a full time job, make sure you take care of some of the planning and shopping on the day off.
- Frozen veggies and fruits are Great. There is a misconception that frozen fruits and vegetables lose their nutrition. That is just not true. These are usually flash frozen while they are at their peak of ripeness, and due to being frozen, that peak is maintained for much longer!
- Machine Tools are Handy. Food processors are love, Food processors are life.
- Store Food Right. Different ingredients like to be stored in different ways. While an ingredient is best stored in the freezer, another might do stored at room temperature. If you're not sure about the best way to store a particular ingredient, google is your friend!
- Internet for The Win. If you can't find that pesky ingredient in a nearby store, check online on amazon. If you can't figure out a cooking procedure by words alone, watch a YouTube video.

ABOUT THE RECIPES

All right! I think we are done with the basics. Let us dive into the recipes! Make sure you read the ingredients and directions carefully before starting a recipe. Make sure you're not allergic to any of the ingredients, and that you have all the tools used in the directions. Let's go!

Smoothies and Drinks

ALMOND BLUEBERRY SMOOTHIE

Time To Prepare: ten minutes

Time to Cook: 0 minutes

Yield: Servings 1

Ingredients:

- 1 banana
- 1 cup frozen blueberries
- 1 tbsp. almond butter
- 1/2 cup almond milk
- Water, as required

Directions:

1. Put in everything to a blender jug.
2. Cover the jug firmly.
3. Blend until the desired smoothness is achieved. Serve and enjoy!

Nutritional Info: Calories: 211 || Fat: 0.2 g || Protein: 5.6 g || Carbohydrates: 3.4 g || Fiber: 2.3 g

ALMOND BUTTER SMOOTHIES

Time To Prepare: five minutes

Time to Cook: 0 minutes

Yield: Servings 1

Ingredients:

- 1 banana, if possible frozen for a creamier shake
- 1 cup of hemp milk

- 1 scoop of hemp protein
- 1 Tablespoon natural almond butter
- few ice cubes

Directions:

Blend all ingredients together and enjoy!

Nutritional Info: Calories: 533 kcal || Protein: 31.23 g || Fat: 26.31 g || Carbohydrates: 47.13 g

---

APPLE CINNAMON WATER

Time To Prepare: five minutes

Time to Cook: five minutes

Yield: Servings 4

Ingredients:

- 1 whole apple, diced
- 5 cinnamon sticks
- Water to cover contents

Directions:

1. Put ingredients in the steamer basket. Put in pot.
2. Put in water cover contents.
3. Secure the lid. Cook on HIGH pressure five minutes.
4. When done, depressurize swiftly.
5. Remove steamer basket. Discard cooked produce.
6. Let flavored water cool. Chill completely before you serve.

Nutritional Info: Calories: 194 || Fat: 0g || Carbohydrates: 12g || Protein: 0g

---

BABY KALE PINEAPPLE SMOOTHIE

Time To Prepare: five minutes

Time to Cook: 0 minutes

Yield: Servings 1

Ingredients:

- 1 cup almond milk
- 1 cup Kale
- 1 tablespoon hemp protein powder
- 1/2 cup frozen pineapple

Directions:

Put the almond milk, pineapple, and greens in the blender and blend until the desired smoothness is achieved.

Nutritional Info: Calories: 389 kcal || Protein: 20.29 g || Fat: 16.2 g || Carbohydrates: 42.29 g

---

BEET AND CHERRY SMOOTHIE

Time To Prepare: five minutes

Time to Cook: 0 minutes

Yield: Servings 4

Ingredients:

- ½ cup frozen cherries, pitted
- ½ teaspoon frozen banana
- 1 tablespoon almond butter
- 10-ounce almond milk, unsweetened
- 2 small beets, peeled and slice into four

Directions:

1. Put in all ingredients in a blender.
2. Blend until the desired smoothness is achieved.

Nutritional Info: Calories 470 || Carbohydrates: 24 g || Fat: 38 g || Protein: 16 g

---

BEET SMOOTHIE

Time To Prepare: ten minutes

Time to Cook: 0 minutes

Yield: Servings 2

Ingredients:

- 1 tbsp. almond butter
- 1/2 banana, peeled and frozen
- 1/2 cup cherries, pitted
- 10 oz. almond milk, unsweetened
- 2 beets, peeled and quartered

Directions:

1. In your blender, combine the milk with the beets, banana, cherries, and butter.
2. Pulse thoroughly, pour into glasses, before you serve. Enjoy!

Nutritional Info: Calories: 165 || Fat: 5 g || Protein: 5 g || Carbohydrates: 22 g || Fiber: 6 g

---

BERRY SHRUB

Time To Prepare: ten minutes

Time to Cook: twenty minutes

Yield: Servings 4

Ingredients:

- ½ a cup of chopped fresh oregano
- 1 cup of dried elderberries
- 2 cups of apple cider vinegar
- 2 cups of honey
- 2 cups of water

Directions:

1. Put in listed ingredients to the instant pot.
2. Secure the lid. Cook on HIGH pressure twenty minutes.
3. When done, depressurize naturally.

4. Pour ingredients through a sieve into a jar.
5. Let cool down. Chill.

Nutritional Info: Calories: 127 || Fat: 0g || Carbohydrates: 6g || Protein: 0g

---

BLACKBERRY & GINGER MILKSHAKE

Time To Prepare: five minutes

Time to Cook: 0 minutes

Yield: Servings 2

Ingredients:

- 1 thumb-sized piece of ginger, grated
- 2 cups of almond milk
- 2 cups of blackberries, washed
- 2 cups of chopped peaches

Directions:

1. Combine all ingredients to a blender or juicer and blend until the desired smoothness is achieved.
2. Serve with a scattering of fresh blackberries and enjoy!

Nutritional Info: Calories: 619 kcal || Protein: fifteen.42 g || Fat: 11.63 g || Carbohydrates: 123.04 g

---

BLACKBERRY ITALIAN DRINK

Time To Prepare: five minutes

Time to Cook: fifteen minutes

Yield: Servings 4

Ingredients:

- 1 bottle sparkling water
- 1 cup blackberries

- 1 lemon, cut
- 2 tbsp. honey

Directions:

1. Put in 1 cup (non-carbonated) water to the instant pot.
2. Put in blackberries to the instant pot.
3. Secure the lid. Cook on HIGH pressure ten minutes.
4. When done, depressurize naturally.
5. Mash the berries in the instant pot. Move to dish. Let cool.
6. As blackberries cook, in a separate small deep cooking pan with a heavy bottom. Put in honey. Simmer five minutes. Cool down.
7. To make the drink. Ladle 1 teaspoon honey. Pour in fruit mixture. Put in carbonated water. Stir.

Nutritional Info: Calories: 249 ‖ Fat: 0.6g ‖ Carbohydrates: 55g ‖ Protein: 7.5g

---

BLENDED COCONUT MILK AND BANANA BREAKFAST SMOOTHIE

Time To Prepare: ten minutes

Time to Cook: 0 minutes

Yield: Servings 4

Ingredients:

- 2 cups almond milk
- 2 cups coconut milk
- 4 ripe moderate-sized bananas
- 4 tbsp. flax seeds
- 4 tsp. cinnamon

Directions:

1. Peel the banana and cut it into ½-inch pieces. Put all the ingredients in the blender and blend into a smoothie.
2. Put in a dash of cinnamon at the top of the smoothie before you serve.

Nutritional Info: Calories: 332 kcal || Protein: 12.49 g || Fat: 14.42 g || Carbohydrates: 42.46 g

---

BLUEBERRY AND SPINACH SHAKE

Time To Prepare: five minutes

Time to Cook: 0 minutes

Yield: Servings 2

Ingredients:

- 1 cup of low-fat Greek yogurt (not necessary)
- 1 cup of organic blueberries (or washed if non-organic)
- 1/2 cup of spinach
- ice cubes to the desired concentration

Directions:

1. Put in ingredients together in a blender until the desired smoothness is achieved and then serve in a tall glass.
2. Drizzle a few fresh berries on top if you prefer!

Nutritional Info: Calories: 233 kcal || Protein: 10.68 g || Fat: 5.38 g || Carbohydrates: 37.13 g

---

BLUEBERRY LIME JUICE

Time To Prepare: five minutes

Time to Cook: five minutes

Yield: Servings 4

Ingredients:

- 1 cup fresh blueberries
- Water to cover contents
- Zest and juice of 1 lime

Directions:

1. Put ingredients in a mesh steamer basket for instant pot. Put in pot.
2. Pour in water to immerse contents.
3. Secure the lid. Cook on HIGH pressure five minutes.
4. When done, depressurize swiftly.
5. Remove steamer basket. Discard cooked produce.
6. Let flavored water cool. Chill completely before you serve.

Nutritional Info: Calories: 86 || Fat: 0g || Carbohydrates: 22g || Protein: 0g

---

BLUEBERRY MATCHA SMOOTHIE

Time To Prepare: five minutes

Time to Cook: 0 minutes

Yield: Servings 2

Ingredients:

- ¼ Teaspoon Ground Cinnamon
- ¼ Teaspoon Ground Ginger
- 1 Banana
- 1 Tablespoon Chia Seeds
- 1 Tablespoon Matcha Powder
- 2 Cups Almond Milk
- 2 Cups Blueberries, Frozen
- 2 Tablespoons Protein Powder, Optional
- A Pinch Sea Salt

Directions:

Blend all ingredients until the desired smoothness is achieved.

Nutritional Info: Calories: 208 || Protein: 8.7 Grams || Fat: 5.7 Grams || Carbohydrates: 31 Grams

---

BLUEBERRY POMEGRANATE SMOOTHIE

Time To Prepare: five minutes

Time to Cook: 0 minutes

Yield: Servings 2

Ingredients:

- ¼ cup of canned coconut milk
- 1 cup of pomegranate juice, unsweetened
- 1 tbsp. of hemp seeds
- 2 cup of frozen blueberries
- 6 to 8 ice cubes

Directions:

1. Mix the smoothie ingredients in your high-speed blender.
2. Pulse the ingredients a few times to cut them up.
3. Combine the mixture on the highest speed setting for thirty to 60 seconds.
4. Pour into glasses and serve.

Nutritional Info: Calories: 282 kcal || Protein: 5.64 g || Fat: 13.8 g || Carbohydrates: 37.75 g

---

BLUEBERRY SMOOTHIE

Time To Prepare: ten minutes

Time to Cook: 0 minutes

Yield: Servings 1

Ingredients:

- 1 banana, peeled
- 1 tbsp. almond butter
- 1 tsp. maca powder
- 1/2 cup almond milk, unsweetened
- 1/2 cup blueberries
- 1/2 cup water
- 1/4 tsp. ground cinnamon
- 2 handfuls baby spinach

Directions:

1. In your blender, combine the spinach with the banana, blueberries, almond butter, cinnamon, maca powder, water, and milk.
2. Pulse thoroughly, pour into a glass, before you serve. Enjoy!

Nutritional Info: Calories: 341 || Fat: 12 g || Protein: 10 g || Carbohydrates: 54 g || Fiber: 12 g

---

BROCCOLI SMOOTHIE

Time To Prepare: five minutes

Time to Cook: 0 minutes

Yield: Servings 4

Ingredients:

- 1 ½ cups strawberries
- 1 ½ cups water
- 1 cup broccoli florets
- 1 cup chopped spinach
- 2 bananas, cut, frozen
- 2 cups frozen mango chunks
- 2 cups pineapple juice

Directions:

1. Combine all ingredients into a blender and blend until the desired smoothness is achieved.
2. Pour into 4 tall glasses before you serve.

Nutritional Info: Calories: 222 kcal || Protein: 3.51 g || Fat: 1.98 g || Carbohydrates: 51.45 g

---

CARROT AND ORANGE TURMERIC DRINK

Time To Prepare: five minutes

Time to Cook: 0 minutes

Yield: Servings 2

Ingredients:

- 1 cup orange juice
- 1 tbsp. lemon juice
- 1/2 inch ginger slice
- 1/4 tsp. turmeric powder
- 2 carrots, peeled, chopped
- 2 tbsp. sugar

Directions:

1. In a blender, put in orange juice, sugar, turmeric powder, carrots, and lemon juice.
2. Blend well.

Serve!

Nutritional Info: Calories: 153 kcal || Protein: 4.47 g || Fat: 3.3 g || Carbohydrates: 27.02 g

CHERRY SMOOTHIE

Time To Prepare: five minutes

Time to Cook: 0 minutes

Yield: Servings 4-6

Ingredients:

- 1 ½ cups vanilla Greek yogurt
- 2 bananas, cut
- 3 cups cherry juice
- 3 cups pitted, froze dark sweet cherries
- Fresh cherries, pitted
- Mint sprigs
- To decorate: Optional

Directions:

1. Combine all ingredients into a blender and blend until the desired smoothness is achieved.
2. Pour into 4 tall glasses.

3. Decorate using optional ingredients if using before you serve.

Nutritional Info: Calories: 114 kcal || Protein: 2.36 g || Fat: 1.88 g || Carbohydrates: 23.49 g

---

CHOCOLATE CHERRY SMOOTHIE

Time To Prepare: five minutes

Time to Cook: 0 minutes

Yield: Servings 2

Ingredients:

- 2 cups almond milk, unsweetened
- 2 dates, pitted, chopped or 2 teaspoons pure maple syrup
- 2 scoops protein powder or 4 tablespoons almond butter (not necessary)
- 4 cups pitted, frozen cherries
- 4 tablespoons cocoa or cacao powder
- Cacao nibs
- Granola
- Hemp hearts
- To serve: Optional

Directions:

1. Combine all ingredients into a blender and blend until the desired smoothness is achieved.
2. Pour into 2 tall glasses and serve topped with optional ingredients.

Nutritional Info: Calories: 339 kcal || Protein: 16.37 g || Fat: 21.34 g || Carbohydrates: 27.99 g

---

CHOCOLATE LATTE WITH REISHI

Time To Prepare: five minutes

Time to Cook: ten minutes

Yield: Servings 2

Ingredients:

- 1 teaspoon Reishi powder
- 2 tablespoons coconut butter
- 4 cups almond milk, unsweetened
- 4 teaspoons raw cacao powder
- A pinch ground cinnamon
- A pinch sea salt
- Sweetener of your choice

Directions:

1. Put in almond milk into a deep cooking pan. Put the deep cooking pan using low heat.
2. When the milk is warm and just starts to bubble, remove the heat. Move into a blender.
3. Put in the remaining ingredients and blend for 30 – 40 seconds or until the desired smoothness is achieved.
4. Pour into mugs before you serve.

Nutritional Info: Calories: 461 kcal || Protein: 19.32 g || Fat: 30.57 g || Carbohydrates: 28.08 g

---

COOKED ICED TEA

Time To Prepare: two minutes

Time to Cook: 4 minutes

Yield: Servings 4

Ingredients:

- 2 tbsp. honey
- 4 regular tea bags
- 6 cups water

Directions:

1. Put in ingredients to the instant pot.
2. Secure the lid. Cook on HIGH pressure 4 minutes.
3. When done, depressurize naturally.

4. Allow to cool to room temperature. Serve over ice.

Nutritional Info: Calories: 22 || Fat: 0g || Carbohydrates: 6g || Protein: 0g

---

CUCUMBER KIWI GREEN SMOOTHIE

Time To Prepare: five minutes

Time to Cook: 0 minutes

Yield: Servings 2

Ingredients:

- ¼ cup of canned coconut milk
- 1 cup of coconut water
- 1 cup of seedless cucumber, chopped
- 2 ripe kiwi fruit
- 2 tbsps. of fresh chopped cilantro
- 6 to 8 ice cubes
- ice cubes

Directions:

1. Mix the smoothie ingredients in your high-speed blender.
2. Pulse the ingredients a few times to cut them up.
3. Combine the mixture on the highest speed setting for thirty to 60 seconds.
4. Pour into glasses and serve.

Nutritional Info: Calories: 140 kcal || Protein: 5.1 g || Fat: 10.52 g || Carbohydrates: 7.4 g

---

CUCUMBER MELON SMOOTHIE

Time To Prepare: five minutes

Time to Cook: 0 minutes

Yield: Servings 2

Ingredients:

- 1 ½ cups of chopped honeydew
- 1 cup of chilled coconut water
- 1 cup of seedless cucumber, diced
- 2 tbsp. of fresh mint
- 6 to 8 ice cubes

Directions:

1. Mix the smoothie ingredients in your high-speed blender.
2. Pulse the ingredients a few times to cut them up.
3. Combine the mixture on the highest speed setting for thirty to 60 seconds.
4. Pour into glasses and serve.

Nutritional Info: Calories: 300 kcal || Protein: 5.83 g || Fat: 8.55 g || Carbohydrates: 51.21 g

DREAMY YUMMY ORANGE CREAM SMOOTHIE

Time To Prepare: five minutes

Time to Cook: 0 minutes

Yield: Servings 2

Ingredients:

- ¼ cup of fresh orange juice
- ½ cup of canned full-fat coconut milk
- 1 cup of almond milk
- 1 navel orange, peel removed
- 6 to 8 ice cubes

Directions:

1. Mix the smoothie ingredients in your high-speed blender.
2. Pulse the ingredients a few times to cut them up.
3. Combine the mixture on the highest speed setting for thirty to 60 seconds.
4. Pour into glasses and serve.

Nutritional Info: Calories: 269 kcal || Protein: 8.63 g || Fat: 21.36 g || Carbohydrates: 12.75 g

FIG SMOOTHIE

Time To Prepare: five minutes

Time to Cook: 0 minutes

Yield: Servings 2

Ingredients:

- 1 Banana
- 1 Cup Almond Milk
- 1 Cup Whole Milk Yogurt, Plain
- 1 Tablespoon Almond Butter
- 1 Teaspoon Flaxseed, Ground
- 1 Teaspoon Honey, Raw
- 3-4 Ice Cubes
- 7 Figs, Halved (Fresh or Frozen)

Directions:

Blend all together ingredients until the desired smoothness is achieved, and serve instantly.

Nutritional Info: Calories: 362 || Protein: 9 Grams || Fat: 12 Grams || Carbohydrates: 60 Grams

FLU FIGHTING TONIC

Time To Prepare: five minutes

Time to Cook: ten minutes

Yield: Servings 2

Ingredients:

- ½ teaspoon turmeric powder
- 2 tablespoons clear honey if possible manuka
- Boiling water, as required
- Juice of 2 lemons
- Lemon slices to decorate

Directions:

1. Split the lemon juice into 2 mugs. Put in ¼ teaspoon turmeric powder into each mug.
2. Put in a tablespoon of honey into each mug.
3. Pour boiling water to fill up the mugs. Stir.
4. Decorate using a slice of lemon before you serve.

Nutritional Info: Calories: 123 kcal || Protein: 3.59 g || Fat: 3.23 g || Carbohydrates: 22.78 g

---

FRESH CRANBERRY AND LIME JUICE

Time To Prepare: five minutes

Time to Cook: 0 minutes

Yield: Servings 2

Ingredients:

- 1/2½ cups of mixed berries (frozen are fine)
- 1/2½ cups of spinach
- 2 limes, juiced
- 4 cups of cranberries

Directions:

Mix all the ingredients with water in a juicer until pureed and serve instantly over ice.

Nutritional Info: Calories: 578 kcal || Protein: 6.83 g || Fat: 9.92 g || Carbohydrates: 119.35 g

---

FRESH TROPICAL JUICE

Time To Prepare: five minutes

Time to Cook: 0 minutes

Yield: Servings 2

Ingredients:

- 1 whole pineapple, peeled and slice into chunks.
- 1 cup of water
- 1/2 can of low-fat coconut milk

Directions:

1. Put in all ingredients to a juicer and blend until the desired smoothness is achieved.
2. Serve over ice.

Nutritional Info: Calories: 116 kcal || Protein: 3.72 g || Fat: 3.13 g || Carbohydrates: 19.55 g

---

GINGER ALE

Time To Prepare: five minutes

Time to Cook: thirty minutes

Yield: Servings 4

Ingredients:

- 1 pound fresh ginger, unpeeled, diced
- 1 quart carbonated water
- 1 tbsp. honey
- Ice for serving
- Juice and rind of 2 lemons
- Lime wedges

Directions:

1. Put ginger and lemon juice in a food processor. Pulse to smooth consistency.
2. Move puree to the instant pot. Mix in honey.
3. Put in lemon peel to the instant pot.
4. Secure the lid. Cook on HIGH pressure thirty minutes.
5. When done, depressurize naturally. Strain and chill.
6. Serve over ice.

Nutritional Info: Calories: 108 || Fat: 0g || Carbohydrates: 28g || Protein: 0g

GINGER, CARROT, AND TURMERIC SMOOTHIE

Time To Prepare: five minutes

Time to Cook: 0 minutes

Yield: Servings 2

Ingredients:

- ½ cup Mango, fresh or frozen chunks
- 1 big Carrot, peeled and chopped
- 1 cup Coconut water
- 1 Orange, peeled and separated
- 1 tbsp. Hemp seeds, raw, shelled
- 1 tsp. Ginger, ground
- 1 tsp. Turmeric, ground
- 1/8 tsp. Cayenne pepper

Directions:

Puree all of the ingredients with one-half cup of ice until the desired smoothness is achieved and drink instantly.

Nutritional Info: Calories 250 || 35 grams sugar || 4.5 grams fat || 7 grams fiber || 48 grams carbs || 6 grams protein

GOLDEN CHAI LATTE

Time To Prepare: five minutes

Time to Cook: ten minutes

Yield: Servings 2

Ingredients:

- ¼ teaspoon ground cinnamon
- ½ cup water
- ½ tablespoon maple syrup
- ½ tablespoon turmeric powder

- 1 ¼ cups cashew milk or any other non-dairy milk of your choice
- 1 teaspoon loose leaf chai tea
- 1/8 teaspoon ground nutmeg
- A pinch ground cardamom

Directions:

1. Put in water and 1-cup milk into a deep cooking pan. Put the deep cooking pan on moderate heat.
2. Put in chai leaves in a tea strainer (the type that that has a lid and you can close). Lower the strainer in the deep cooking pan. Put in spices.
3. When it just comes to a light boil, remove the heat. Allow it to cool for five minutes. Take out the tea strainer and discard the leaves.
4. Put in maple syrup and stir.
5. Pour into glasses. Sprinkle remaining cashew milk on top. Decorate using cinnamon and nutmeg before you serve.

Nutritional Info: Calories: 142 kcal || Protein: 8.59 g || Fat: 6.26 g || Carbohydrates: 13.3 g

---

GREEN VANILLA SMOOTHIE

Time To Prepare: ten minutes

Time to Cook: 0 minutes

Yield: Servings 1

Ingredients:

- 1 1/2 cups fresh spinach leaves
- 1 banana, cut in chunks
- 1 cup grapes
- 1 tub (6 oz.) vanilla yogurt
- 1/2 apple, cored and chopped

Directions:

1. Put in everything to a blender jug.
2. Cover the jug firmly.
3. Blend until the desired smoothness is achieved. Serve and enjoy!

Nutritional Info: Calories: 131 || Fat: 0.2 g || Protein: 2.6 g || Carbohydrates: 9.1 g || Fiber: 1.3 g

---

HIBISCUS TEA

Time To Prepare: five minutes

Time to Cook: ten minutes

Yield: Servings 4

Ingredients:

- 1 tbsp. honey
- 1 tsp fresh ginger, grated
- 10 cups water
- 2 cup dried hibiscus petals
- Rind from 1 pineapple

Directions:

1. Wash hibiscus leaves meticulously with cold water.
2. Take away the dust.
3. Put in water, honey, and ginger to the instant pot. Stir.
4. Mix in hibiscus petals and pineapple rind.
5. Secure the lid. Cook on HIGH pressure ten minutes.
6. When done, depressurize naturally.
7. Remove pineapple rind. Pass liquid through a fine-mesh strainer.
8. Cool thoroughly. Chill before you serve.

Nutritional Info: Calories: 114 || Fat: 0g || Carbohydrates: 28g || Protein: 0g

---

HOT APPLE CIDER

Time To Prepare: five minutes

Time to Cook: fifteen minutes

Yield: Servings 4

Ingredients:

- ½ cup fresh cranberries
- ½ cup honey
- ½ star of anise
- ½ tsp whole cloves
- 1 lemon, peeled, cut into segments
- 1 orange, peeled, cut into segments
- 2 cinnamon sticks
- 7 medium apples, cored, quarter
- Water to cover ingredients

Directions:

1. Put in apples, lemon, orange, and cranberries to the instant pot.
2. Put in cinnamon stick, star anise, and cloves.
3. Pour in water to immerse ingredients.
4. Secure the lid. Cook on HIGH pressure fifteen minutes.
5. Depressurize naturally.
6. Mash fruit using a masher to release juices.
7. Strain the liquid. Chill completely before you serve.

Nutritional Info: Calories: 153 || Fat: 9g || Carbohydrates: 14g || Protein: 4g

---

HOT PEPPERMINT VANILLA LATTE

Time To Prepare: five minutes

Time to Cook: five minutes

Yield: Servings 4

Ingredients:

- ¼ cup honey
- 1 tsp vanilla
- 2 cups coffee
- 23 drops peppermint oil
- 4 cups almond milk

Directions:

1. Put in listed ingredients to the instant pot.
2. Secure the lid. Cook on HIGH pressure five minutes.
3. When done, depressurize naturally.
4. Serve warm.

Nutritional Info: Calories: 279 || Fat: 3g || Carbohydrates: 61g || Protein: 3g

---

INSTANT HORCHATA

Time To Prepare: five minutes

Time to Cook: five minutes

Yield: Servings 4

Ingredients:

- 1 cinnamon stick, broken into little chunks
- 32 ounces rice milk
- 6 tbsp. honey

Directions:

1. Put in listed ingredients to the instant pot.
2. Secure the lid. Cook on HIGH pressure five minutes.
3. When done, depressurize naturally over ten minutes.
4. Cool thoroughly. Chill before you serve.

Nutritional Info: Calories: 226 || Fat: 1g || Carbohydrates: 53g || Protein: 2g

---

JAMAICAN HIBISCUS TEA

Time To Prepare: five minutes

Time to Cook: five minutes

Yield: Servings 4

Ingredients:

- ½ tsp ginger, minced
- 1 cup dried hibiscus flowers
- 1 tbsp. honey
- 8 cups water
- Ice as required
- Juice of 1 lime

Directions:

1. Put in hibiscus flowers, water, honey, and ginger to the instant pot.
2. Secure the lid. Cook on HIGH pressure five minutes.
3. When done, depressurize naturally.
4. Cool thoroughly. Move to glass decanter. Mix in lime Juice. Pour over ice.

Nutritional Info: Calories: 197 || Fat: 0g || Carbohydrates: 18g || Protein: 0g

---

KALE SMOOTHIE

Time To Prepare: ten minutes

Time to Cook: 0 minutes

Yield: Servings 2

Ingredients:

- 10 kale leaves
- 2 pears, chopped
- 5 bananas, peeled and slice into chunks
- 5 cups almond milk
- 5 tbsp. almond butter

Directions:

1. In your blender, combine the kale with the bananas, pears, almond butter, and almond milk.
2. Pulse thoroughly, split into glasses, before you serve. Enjoy!

Nutritional Info: Calories: 267 || Fat: 11 g || Protein: 7 g || Carbohydrates: fifteen g || Fiber: 7 g

KIWI STRAWBERRY SMOOTHIE

Time To Prepare: ten minutes

Time to Cook: 0 minutes

Yield: Servings 1

Ingredients:

- ¼ cup Chia seed powder
- ½ cup Strawberries, fresh or frozen, chopped
- 1 Banana, diced
- 1 cup Milk, almond or coconut
- 1 Kiwi, peeled and chopped
- 1 tsp. Basil, ground
- 1 tsp. Turmeric, ground

Directions:

Drink instantly after all the ingredients have been thoroughly combined.

Nutritional Info: Calories 250 || 9.9 grams sugar || 1 gram fat || 34 grams carbs || 4.3 grams fiber ||

LEMON GINGER ICED TEA

Time To Prepare: five minutes

Time to Cook: ten minutes

Yield: Servings 2-3

Ingredients:

- ¼ teaspoon turmeric
- 1 tablespoon fresh lemon juice or to taste (not necessary)
- 1 tablespoon maple syrup
- 2 – 3 lemon slices
- 2 inches fresh ginger, peeled, thinly cut or to taste
- 3-4 cups water

- A pinch ground cinnamon

Directions:

1. Pour water into a deep cooking pan. Put in ginger, turmeric, lemon slices, and cinnamon. Put the deep cooking pan on moderate heat.
2. Cover and simmer for eight - ten minutes.
3. Strain and pour into a jar. Place the maple syrup, and lemon juice, then stir. Chill for eight – 10 hours.
4. Stir thoroughly. Pour into glasses before you serve.

Nutritional Info: Calories: 55 kcal || Protein: 2.32 g || Fat: 2.13 g || Carbohydrates: 7.47 g

MANGO AND GINGER INFUSED WATER

Time To Prepare: five minutes

Time to Cook: five minutes

Yield: Servings 4

Ingredients:

- 1 cup fresh mango, chopped
- 2-inch piece ginger, peeled, cubed
- Water to cover ingredients

Directions:

1. Put ingredients in the mesh steamer basket.
2. Put basket in the instant pot.
3. Put in water to immerse contents.
4. Secure the lid. Cook on HIGH pressure five minutes.
5. When done, depressurize swiftly.
6. Remove steamer basket. Discard cooked produce.
7. Let flavored water cool. Chill completely and serve.

Nutritional Info: Calories: 209 || Fat: 1g || Carbohydrates: 51g || Protein: 2g

MANGO TOMATO SMOOTHIE

Time To Prepare: five minutes

Time to Cook: 0 minutes

Yield: Servings 4

Ingredients:

- 1 cup almond milk
- 2 cups chopped cilantro
- 2 cups pineapple chunks
- 2 mangoes, peeled, pitted
- 4 Campari tomatoes, chopped
- 6 cups fresh baby spinach

Directions:

1. Combine all ingredients into a blender and blend until the desired smoothness is achieved.
2. Pour into 4 tall glasses before you serve.

Nutritional Info: Calories: 395 kcal || Protein: 13.1 g || Fat: 8.19 g || Carbohydrates: 73.65 g

---

MIXED FRUIT & NUT MILKSHAKE

Time To Prepare: five minutes

Time to Cook: 0 minutes

Yield: Servings 2

Ingredients:

- 1 tbsp. of honey
- 1/2 cup of almond milk
- 1½ grapefruit; peeled and chopped
- 1/2½ inch piece of ginger, minced
- 12 strawberries
- 2 tbsp. of chopped almonds
- juice of 1 orange

Directions:

1. Put everything but the strawberries in a blender until the desired smoothness is achieved.
2. Put in in the strawberries and blend until pureed, serving in a tall glass.

Nutritional Info: Calories: 140 kcal || Protein: 5.89 g || Fat: 5.84 g || Carbohydrates: 17.36 g

---

PARSLEY GINGER GREEN JUICE

Time To Prepare: five minutes

Time to Cook: 0 minutes

Yield: Servings 2

Ingredients:

- 2 cucumbers, chopped
- 2 green apples, cored
- 2 lemons, peeled, halved
- 4 cups chopped parsley
- 4 cups chopped spinach
- 4 inches fresh ginger, peeled, cut
- 6 stalks celery, chopped

Directions:

1. Juice together all the ingredients in a juicer.
2. Pour into 2 glasses before you serve.

Nutritional Info: Calories: 239 kcal || Protein: 10.74 g || Fat: 5.08 g || Carbohydrates: 44.86 g

---

PEACH AND RASPBERRY LEMONADE

Time To Prepare: five minutes

Time to Cook: five minutes

Yield: Servings 4

Ingredients:

- ½ cup fresh raspberries
- 1 cup fresh peaches, chopped
- Water to cover ingredients
- Zest and juice of 1 lemon

Directions:

1. Put ingredients in mesh basket for instant pot. Put in pot.
2. Put in water to barely cover the fruit.
3. Secure the lid. Cook on HIGH pressure five minutes.
4. When done, depressurize swiftly.
5. Remove steamer basket. Discard cooked produce.
6. Let flavored water cool. Chill completely before you serve.

Nutritional Info: Calories: 77 || Fat: 0g || Carbohydrates: 19g || Protein: 0g

---

PEACH MAPLE SMOOTHIE

Time To Prepare: ten minutes

Time to Cook: 0 minutes

Yield: Servings 1

Ingredients:

- 1 cup fat-free yogurt
- 1 cup ice
- 2 tbsp. maple syrup
- 4 big peaches, peeled and chopped

Directions:

1. Put in everything to a blender jug.
2. Cover the jug firmly.
3. Blend until the desired smoothness is achieved. Serve and enjoy!

Nutritional Info: Calories: 125 || Fat: 0.4 g || Protein: 5.6 g || Carbohydrates: 8 g || Fiber: 2.3 g

PEACHY KEEN SMOOTHIE

Time To Prepare: five minutes

Time to Cook: 0 minutes

Yield: Servings 2

Ingredients:

- 1 ½ cups of frozen peaches
- 1 cup of almond milk
- 1 small frozen banana
- 2 tbsp. of raw hemp seeds
- 6 to 8 ice cubes
- Pinch of ground ginger

Directions:

1. Mix the smoothie ingredients in your high-speed blender.
2. Pulse the ingredients a few times to cut them up.
3. Combine the mixture on the highest speed setting for thirty to 60 seconds.
4. Pour into glasses and serve.

Nutritional Info: Calories: 388 kcal || Protein: 10.59 g || Fat: 11.93 g || Carbohydrates: 64.08 g

PINEAPPLE & GINGER JUICE

Time To Prepare: five minutes

Time to Cook: 0 minutes

Yield: Servings 2

Ingredients:

- 2 apples, cored, chopped
- 2 cucumbers, chopped
- 2 cups chopped pineapple
- 2 cups spinach
- 2 inches ginger, peeled, cut

- 2 lemons, peeled, halved
- 8 celery stalks, chopped

Directions:

1. Juice together all the ingredients in a juicer.
2. Pour into 2 glasses before you serve.

Nutritional Info: Calories: 339 kcal || Protein: 7.44 g || Fat: 4.23 g || Carbohydrates: 75.38 g

PINEAPPLE AND GREENS SMOOTHIE

Time To Prepare: five minutes

Time to Cook: 0 minutes

Yield: Servings 2

Ingredients:

- ¾ cup of almond milk
- 1 cup of chopped spinach
- 1 cup of frozen pineapple
- 1 small frozen banana
- 1 tbsp. of honey
- 2 tbsp. Of chia seeds

Directions:

1. Mix the smoothie ingredients in your high-speed blender.
2. Pulse the ingredients a few times to cut them up.
3. Combine the mixture on the highest speed setting for thirty to 60 seconds.
4. Pour into glasses and serve.

Nutritional Info: Calories: 272 kcal || Protein: 5.27 g || Fat: 4.5 g || Carbohydrates: 56.37 g

PINEAPPLE- GINGER SMOOTHIE

Time To Prepare: five minutes

Time to Cook: 0 minutes

Yield: Servings 1

Ingredients:

- ½ inch thick ginger, cut
- 1 cup coconut milk
- 1 cup pineapple slice

Directions:

1. Put all ingredients in a blender.
2. Pulse until the desired smoothness is achieved.
3. Chill before you serve.

Nutritional Info: Calories 299 || Fat: 8 g || Protein: 9 g || Carbohydrates: 51 g

---

PINEAPPLE SMOOTHIE

Time To Prepare: ten minutes

Time to Cook: 0 minutes

Yield: Servings 2

Ingredients:

- 1 1/2 cups pineapple chunks
- 1 cup coconut water
- 1 orange, peeled and slice into quarters
- 1 tbsp. fresh grated ginger
- 1 tsp. chia seeds
- 1 tsp. turmeric powder
- A pinch black pepper

Directions:

1. In your blender, combine the coconut water with the orange, pineapple, ginger, chia seeds, turmeric, and black pepper.
2. Pulse thoroughly, pour into a glass.

Makes for a great breakfast!

Nutritional Info: Calories: 151 || Fat: 2 g || Protein: 4 g || Carbohydrates: 12 g || Fiber: 6 g

---

PINK CALIFORNIA SMOOTHIE

Time To Prepare: ten minutes

Time to Cook: 0 minutes

Yield: Servings 1

Ingredients:

- 1 container (8 oz.) lemon yogurt
- 1/3 cup orange juice
- 7 big strawberries

Directions:

1. Put in everything to a blender jug.
2. Cover the jug firmly.
3. Blend until the desired smoothness is achieved. Serve and enjoy!

Nutritional Info: Calories: 144 || Fat: 0.4 g || Protein: 5.6 g || Carbohydrates: 8 g || Fiber: 2.3 g

---

PUMPKIN PIE SMOOTHIE

Time To Prepare: five minutes

Time to Cook: 0 minutes

Yield: Servings 2

Ingredients:

- ½ Cup Pumpkin, Canned & Unsweetened
- 1 Banana
- 1 Cup Almond Milk
- 1 Teaspoon Ground Cinnamon

- 1 Teaspoon Ground Nutmeg
- 1 Teaspoon Maple Syrup, Pure
- 1 Teaspoon Vanilla Extract Pure
- 2 Tablespoons Almond Butter, Heaping
- 2-3 Ice Cubes

Directions:

Blend all ingredients together until the desired smoothness is achieved.

Nutritional Info: Calories: 235 || Protein: 5.6 Grams || Fat: 11 Grams || Carbohydrates: 27.8 Grams

---

PURPLE FRUIT SMOOTHIE

Time To Prepare: ten minutes

Time to Cook: 0 minutes

Yield: Servings 1

Ingredients:

- 2 frozen bananas, cut in chunks
- 1 cup orange juice
- 1 tbsp. honey, optional
- 1 tsp. vanilla extract, optional
- 1/2 cup frozen blueberries

Directions:

1. Put in everything to a blender jug.
2. Cover the jug firmly.
3. Blend until the desired smoothness is achieved. Serve and enjoy!

Nutritional Info: Calories: 133 || Fat: 1.1 g || Protein: 3.6 g || Carbohydrates: 7.6 g || Fiber: 1.3 g

---

RASPBERRY BANANA SMOOTHIE

Time To Prepare: ten minutes

Time to Cook: 0 minutes

Yield: Servings 1

Ingredients:

- 1 banana
- 1 cup almond milk
- 1 cup frozen raspberries
- 1 cup raspberry yogurt
- 1 tbsp. flaxseed meal
- 1/4 cup Concord grape juice
- 1/4 cup rolled oats
- 16 whole almonds

Directions:

1. Put in everything to a blender jug.
2. Cover the jug firmly.
3. Blend until the desired smoothness is achieved and then serve. Enjoy!

Nutritional Info: Calories: 214 || Fat: 0.4 g || Protein: 5.6 g || Carbohydrates: 8 g || Fiber: 2.3 g

---

RASPBERRY SMOOTHIE

Time To Prepare: ten minutes

Time to Cook: 0 minutes

Yield: Servings 2

Ingredients:

- 1 avocado, pitted and peeled
- 1/2 cup raspberries
- 3/4 cup raspberry juice
- 3/4 cup orange juice

Directions:

1. In your blender, combine the avocado with the raspberry juice, orange juice, and raspberries.
2. Pulse thoroughly, split into 2 glasses, before you serve. Enjoy!

Nutritional Info: Calories: 125 || Fat: 11 g || Protein: 3 g || Carbohydrates: 9 g || Fiber: 7 g

---

SPICY TOMATO SMOOTHIE

Time To Prepare: five minutes

Time to Cook: 0 minutes

Yield: Servings 2

Ingredients:

- ¼ cup chopped red onion
- 1 jalapeño, cut, deseed if you wish
- 1 small bunch cilantro, chopped
- 1 small cucumber
- 2 big carrots, chopped
- 2 cloves garlic, peeled
- 6 small vine tomatoes
- Juice of 2 limes

Directions:

1. Combine all ingredients into a blender and blend until the desired smoothness is achieved.
2. Pour into 2 tall glasses before you serve.

Nutritional Info: Calories: 269 kcal || Protein: 24.87 g || Fat: 8.71 g || Carbohydrates: 26.89 g

---

STRAWBERRY OATMEAL SMOOTHIE

Time To Prepare: ten minutes

Time to Cook: 0 minutes

Yield: Servings 1

Ingredients:

- 1 cup soy milk
- 1 banana, broken into chunks
- 14 frozen strawberries
- 1/2 cup rolled oats
- 1/2 tsp. vanilla extract
- 1 1/2 tsp. honey

Directions:

1. Put in everything to a blender jug.
2. Cover the jug firmly.
3. Blend until the desired smoothness is achieved. Serve and enjoy!

Nutritional Info: Calories: 172 || Fat: 0.4 g || Protein: 5.6 g || Carbohydrates: 8 g || Fiber: 2 g

---

SWEET & SAVOURY SMOOTHIE

Time To Prepare: five minutes

Time to Cook: 0 minutes

Yield: Servings 2

Ingredients:

- 1 apple, peeled and cut
- 1 banana, peeled and cut
- 1 cup of almond or soy milk
- 1 cup of fresh pineapple, peeled and cut
- 1 tbsp. of lemon juice
- 1/2 tbsp. of ginger, grated
- 1/4 tsp of ground turmeric
- 2 cups of carrots, peeled and cut
- 2 cups of filtered water.

Directions:

1. Blend carrots and water to make a pureed carrot juice.
2. Pour into a Mason jar or sealable container, cover, and store in the refrigerator.

3. When done, put in the rest of the smoothie ingredients to a blender or juicer until the desired smoothness is achieved.
4. Put in the carrot juice in at the end, blending meticulously until the desired smoothness is achieved.
5. Serve with or without ice.

Nutritional Info: Calories: 225 kcal || Protein: 6.03 g || Fat: 5.78 g || Carbohydrates: 39.93 g

---

SWEET CRANBERRY JUICE

Time To Prepare: five minutes

Time to Cook: 8 minutes

Yield: Servings 4

Ingredients:

- ½ cup honey
- 1 cinnamon stick
- 1 gallon filtered water
- 4 cups fresh cranberries
- Juice of 1 lemon

Directions:

1. Put in cranberries, ½ of water, cinnamon cling to the instant pot.
2. Secure the lid. Cook on HIGH pressure 8 minutes.
3. Depressurize naturally.
4. Once cool, strain liquid. Put in remaining water.
5. Mix in honey and lemon. Cool thoroughly.
6. Chill before you serve.

Nutritional Info: Calories: 184 || Fat: 0g || Carbohydrates: 49g || Protein: 1g

---

TRIPLE FRUIT SMOOTHIE

Time To Prepare: ten minutes

Time to Cook: 0 minutes

Yield: Servings 1

Ingredients:

- 1 banana, peeled and chopped
- 1 container (8 oz.) peach yogurt
- 1 cup ice cubes
- 1 cup strawberries
- 1 kiwi, cut
- 1/2 cup blueberries
- 1/2 cup orange juice

Directions:

1. Put in everything to a blender jug.
2. Cover the jug firmly.
3. Blend until the desired smoothness is achieved. Serve and enjoy!

Nutritional Info: Calories: 124 || Fat: 0.4 g || Protein: 5.6 g || Carbohydrates: 8 g || Fiber: 2.3 g

TROPICAL MANGO COCONUT SMOOTHIE

Time To Prepare: five minutes

Time to Cook: 0 minutes

Yield: Servings 2

Ingredients:

- ½ cup of canned coconut milk
- ½ cup of fresh orange juice
- 1 ½ cups of frozen mango
- 1 ½ tsp of honey
- 1 medium frozen banana
- 1 tbsp. of fresh lemon juice

Directions:

1. Mix the smoothie ingredients in your high-speed blender.
2. Pulse the ingredients a few times to cut them up.

3. Combine the mixture on the highest speed setting for thirty to 60 seconds.
4. Pour into glasses and serve.

Nutritional Info: Calories: 354 kcal || Protein: 6.7 g || Fat: 18.09 g || Carbohydrates: 47.42 g

---

TROPICAL PINEAPPLE KIWI SMOOTHIE

Time To Prepare: five minutes

Time to Cook: 0 minutes

Yield: Servings 2

Ingredients:

- 1 ½ cup of frozen pineapple
- 1 cup of canned full-fat coconut milk
- 1 ripe kiwi; peeled and chopped
- 1 tsp of spirulina powder
- 3 tsp of lime juice
- 6 to 8 ice cubes

Directions:

1. Mix the smoothie ingredients in your high-speed blender.
2. Pulse the ingredients a few times to cut them up.
3. Combine the mixture on the highest speed setting.
4. Pour into glasses and serve.

Nutritional Info: Calories: 480 kcal || Protein: 7.38 g || Fat: 31.92 g || Carbohydrates: 48.35 g

---

TURMERIC AND GINGER TONIC

Time To Prepare: five minutes

Time to Cook: ten minutes

Yield: Servings 4

Ingredients:

- 1/8 teaspoon cayenne pepper
- 2 tablespoons grated, fresh ginger
- 2 tablespoons grated, fresh turmeric
- 6 cups water
- Juice of 2 lemons
- Maple syrup or honey to taste
- The rind of 2 lemons, peeled

Directions:

1. Put in water, ginger, turmeric, cayenne pepper, and lemon rind into a deep cooking pan.
2. Put the deep cooking pan on moderate to high heat. (Do not boil)
3. Once the mixture is hot, remove from heat.
4. Strain into 4 mugs. Put in honey and lemon juice and stir.
5. Serve warm.

Nutritional Info: Calories: 48 kcal || Protein: 2.28 g || Fat: 1.81 g || Carbohydrates: 7.03 g

---

TURMERIC DELIGHT

Time To Prepare: five minutes

Time to Cook: 0 minutes

Yield: Servings 2

Ingredients:

- ¼ Teaspoon Ginger
- ½ Teaspoon Cinnamon
- 1 Banana, Sliced
- 1 Tablespoon Lemon Juice, Fresh
- 1 Teaspoon Turmeric
- 2 Cups Yogurt, Plain & Whole Milk
- 2 Teaspoons Honey, Raw

Directions:

Combine all ingredients into a blender then blend until the desired smoothness is achieved.

Nutritional Info: Calories: 234 || Protein: 9.3 Grams || Fat: 8.2 Grams || Carbohydrates: 33.5 Grams

---

TURMERIC HOT CHOCOLATE

Time To Prepare: five minutes

Time to Cook: ten minutes

Yield: Servings 2

Ingredients:

- 1/8 tsp. cayenne pepper, optional
- 1/8 tsp. pepper
- 2 cups milk
- 2 tsp. ground turmeric
- 3 tbsp. cacao or cocoa powder
- 4 tsp. coconut oil
- 4 tsp. honey

Directions:

1. Put in milk, turmeric, cocoa, and coconut oil into a deep cooking pan. Put the deep cooking pan on moderate heat. Coconut oil and pepper are added because it helps to absorb the turmeric.
2. Whisk regularly until well blended.
3. When it starts to boil, remove from heat. Put in honey, cayenne pepper, and pepper and whisk well.
4. Split into 2 cups before you serve.

Nutritional Info: Calories: 339 kcal || Protein: 12.76 g || Fat: 21.19 g || Carbohydrates: 30.35 g

---

TURMERIC TEA

Time To Prepare: five minutes

Time to Cook: fifteen minutes

Yield: Servings 2

Ingredients:

- ½ teaspoon ground ginger
- ½ teaspoon turmeric powder
- ½ tsp ground cinnamon
- 2 cups water
- 2 lemon juices
- 2 tablespoons honey

Directions:

1. Put in water into a deep cooking pan. Put the deep cooking pan on moderate heat.
2. When it starts to boil, put in turmeric, cinnamon, and ginger and stir slowly.
3. Remove the heat. Cover and allow the mixture to steep for 12 – fifteen minutes. Put in honey and lemon juice.
4. Stir and pour into mugs.
5. Serve.

Nutritional Info: Calories: 121 kcal || Protein: 3.57 g || Fat: 3.2 g || Carbohydrates: 21.97 g

VANILLA AVOCADO SMOOTHIE

Time To Prepare: ten minutes

Time to Cook: 0 minutes

Yield: Servings 1

Ingredients:

- 1 cup almond milk
- 1 ripe avocado, halved and pitted
- 1/2 cup vanilla yogurt
- 3 tbsp. honey
- 8 ice cubes

Directions:

1. Put in everything to a blender jug.
2. Cover the jug firmly.
3. Blend until the desired smoothness is achieved. Serve and enjoy!

Nutritional Info: Calories: 143 || Fat: 1.2 g || Protein: 4.6 g || Carbohydrates: 21 g || Fiber: 2.3 g

---

VANILLA BLUEBERRY SMOOTHIE

Time To Prepare: five minutes

Time to Cook: 0 minutes

Yield: Servings 1

Ingredients:

- 1 cup fresh blueberries
- 1 tbsp. flaxseed oil
- 2 cups hemp milk
- 2 tbsp. hemp protein powder
- Handful of ice/ 1 cup frozen blueberries

Directions:

1. Mix milk and fresh blueberries plus ice (or frozen blueberries) in a blender.
2. Blend for a minute, move to a glass, and mix in flaxseed oil.

Nutritional Info: Calories: 1041 kcal || Protein: 35.21 g || Fat: 41.04 g || Carbohydrates: 140.4 g

---

VANILLA TURMERIC ORANGE JUICE

Time To Prepare: five minutes

Time to Cook: 0 minutes

Yield: Servings 2

Ingredients:

- ½ teaspoon turmeric powder
- 1 teaspoon ground cinnamon
- 2 cups unsweetened almond milk
- 2 teaspoons vanilla extract

- 6 oranges, peeled, separated into segments, deseeded
- Pepper to taste

Directions:

1. Juice the oranges. Put in the remaining ingredients.
2. Pour into 2 glasses before you serve.

Nutritional Info: Calories: 223 kcal || Protein: 11.47 g || Fat: 11.79 g || Carbohydrates: fifteen.9 g

---

VOLUPTUOUS VANILLA HOT DRINK

Time To Prepare: ten minutes

Time to Cook: 0 minutes

Yield: Servings 1

Ingredients:

- 1 scoop of hemp protein
- 1/2 Tbsp. ground cinnamon (or more to taste)
- 1/2 Tbsp. vanilla extract
- 3 cups unsweetened almond milk (or 1 1/2 cup full-fat coconut milk + 1 1/2 cups water)
- Stevia to taste

Directions:

1. Put the almond milk into a pitcher. Put ground cinnamon, hemp, vanilla extract in a small deep cooking pan on moderate to high heat. Heat until the pure liquid stevia is just melted and then pour the pure liquid stevia mixture into the pitcher.
2. Stir until the pure liquid stevia is well blended with the almond milk. Bring the pitcher in your refrigerator and let it cool for minimum two hours. Stir thoroughly before you serve.

Nutritional Info: Calories: 656 kcal || Protein: 42.12 g || Fat: 33.05 g || Carbohydrates: 44.45 g

WASSAIL

Time To Prepare: five minutes

Time to Cook: ten minutes

Yield: Servings 4

Ingredients:

- ½ tsp nutmeg
- 1 inch peeled ginger
- 10 cloves
- 2 vanilla beans, split or 2 Tbsp pure vanilla extract
- 4 cups orange juice
- 5 cinnamon sticks
- 8 cups apple cider
- Zest and juice of 2 lemons

Directions:

1. Pour cider and orange juice in the instant pot.
2. Put cinnamon sticks, nutmeg piece, cloves, lemon zest, vanilla beans in the steamer basket.
3. If you didn't use vanilla beans, pour in vanilla extract. Put in lemon juice.
4. Secure the lid. Cook on HIGH pressure ten minutes.
5. When done, depressurize naturally.
6. Discard contents of the steamer basket.
7. Serve hot from the pot.

Nutritional Info: Calories: 221 || Fat: 0g || Carbohydrates: 42g || Protein: 0g

WHITE HOT CHOCOLATE

Time To Prepare: five minutes

Time to Cook: six minutes

Yield: Servings 2

Ingredients:

- ¼ cup cocoa powder/butter
- 2 - 2½ Tbsp honey
- 2 tsp vanilla extract
- 3 cups coconut milk
- Pinch of sea salt

Directions:

1. Put in milk, cocoa powder/butter, honey, vanilla extract, and salt to the instant pot.
2. Secure the lid. Cook on LOW pressure six minutes.
3. Depressurize swiftly.
4. Use a hand blender to blend contents 25 seconds.
5. Serve hot.

Nutritional Info: Calories: 331 || Fat: 14g || Carbohydrates: 47g || Protein: 4g

---

WONDERFUL WATERMELON DRINK

Time To Prepare: five minutes

Time to Cook: 0 minutes

Yield: Servings 2

Ingredients:

- 1 cup of coconut water
- 1 cup of watermelon chunks
- 1/2 cup of tart cherries
- 2 cups of frozen mixed berries
- 2 tbsp. of chia seeds

Directions:

1. Combine all ingredients in a blender or juicer then blend until pureed.
2. Serve instantly and enjoy!

Nutritional Info: Calories: 330 kcal || Protein: 10.22 g || Fat: 9.71 g || Carbohydrates: 53.3 g

ZESTY CITRUS SMOOTHIE

Time To Prepare: five minutes

Time to Cook: 0 minutes

Yield: Servings 1

Ingredients:

- 1 cup almond milk
- 1 med orange peeled, cleaned, and cut into sections
- 1 tbsp. flaxseed oil
- 2 tsp hemp protein powder
- half cup lemon juice
- Handful of ice

Directions:

1. Mix milk, lemon juice, orange, and ice in a blender.
2. Blend for a minute, move to a glass, and mix in flaxseed oil.

Nutritional Info: Calories: 427 kcal || Protein: 17.5 g || Fat: 28.88 g || Carbohydrates: 24.96 g

ABOUT THE AUTHOR

Stephanie Bennett is an American health coach, foodie, and author based in New York. She enjoys sharing simple, delicious recipes with her readers, and coming up with new ways to help people live a healthier life.